French Lessons

poems by

Roberta Hatcher

Finishing Line Press
Georgetown, Kentucky

French Lessons

ACKNOWLEDGMENTS

Poems in this book have appeared or are forthcoming, sometimes in
earlier versions, in the following publications, to whose editors grateful
acknowledgement is made:

Comstock Review: "Household: Object Lesson"
Main Street Rag: "In the Lake Superior Winter"
Pittsburgh City Paper: "The Washing-Machine Stream"
Pittsburgh Post-Gazette: "Thank you for Crawling"
Storm Cellar: "American Notebook"
St. Petersburg Review: "French Lesson #3: Le temps du verbe"
Voices from the Attic: "Langue étrangère" and "The Need for Building"

Publisher: Leah Maines

Editor: Christen Kincaid

Cover Art: Photo by Roberta Hatcher, "Le Nouveau Petit Robert: Dictionnaire de
la Langue Française"

Author Photo: Ruth E. Hendricks

Cover Design: Elizabeth Maines

Printed in the USA on acid-free paper.
Order online: www.finishinglinepress.com
        also available on amazon.com

Author inquiries and mail orders:
Finishing Line Press
P. O. Box 1626
Georgetown, Kentucky 40324
U. S. A.

Table of Contents

For Marc

Langue étrangère

Boldly, as we stood
talking in broad daylight,
the young stranger leaned over
and stuck his tongue down my throat.

The cheek!
What made him think I would let him
get away with it?
Such a public undoing . . .

I was too young then
to understand what was happening . . .

        of course I

let him
      get   a way

      with   it

now

          every encounter

      brings an/other

         sweet little death

Household: Object Lesson

"And now with some pleasure I find that it's seven; and must cook dinner. Haddock and sausage meat. I think it is true that one gains a certain hold on sausage and haddock by writing them down."

Virginia Woolf, A Writer's Diary, Sunday, March 8th, 1941

Wndow—
Warm days I lean out.
I don't even mind
the dust on my white sleeve elbow.

Books—
I no longer touch them.
They lean for company,
strain to hold each other up.

Pillow—
It bears the trace
of every head laid down on it,
texture with no discernible pattern.

Quilt—
From my own body comes
this captured heat
multiplied a hundred-fold.

Countertop—
We cook, we eat,
we do the dishes.
Sometimes we just cook and eat.

Poinsettia—
Something about blooming
in darkened rooms.
Passion erupts on my tabletop.

Calendar—
Despite the new year
now two weeks old,
I am reluctant to turn it over.

Newspaper—
Countless thousands dead in Iraq,
the work of my country's government.
I slowly fold the paper for recycling.

Desklamp—
How sweet the memory
of walking down roads
not knowing where the future lay.

Door—
then stairway, and below,
the street. We go out
so far, we return.

American Notebook

Below my window
people are singing,
it's a party across the street.
After the first line they
don't know the words—
da da da *da* da da *da da* . . .
The voices drift apart—
they don't know the tune either.
Sometimes wanting
is not enough.

*

We are driving down the highway
and you know the words to every song.
The windows frost up
with the wetness of our breath,
like music made visible
before, laughing, we wipe it away.
The car rolls like a cloud
over the Minnesota plain.
I wonder if you ever
think of that day.

*

We sit undressed at your kitchen table,
we've been sitting here three days.
Afternoon of pot and opera, then brandy,
cigarettes, now two remaining Marlboros mark the end.
I had brought you a tape, Keith Jarrett at Köln.
A man alone with a piano.
The music holds, withholds—
one moment as he plays he softly moans.
You teach me how to listen, like an initiation:
sex is everywhere, the square root of everything.

I've come alone to Avignon,
soothed after travel
by cool shower, smooth sheets on my skin.
In the room next door heels clickclick on the floor
moving with purpose like European women do.
Then I hear laughter and the sound of young women,
singing *Where Have All the Flowers Gone*
in German.
Everything here is like that—
familiar yet strange.

*

Last week in a movie I heard *Beyond the Sea*
in French, taking me back to the bar
on the lake, that summer, that jukebox,
that dance we should never have danced.
Now I learn that *Beyond the Sea*
was written first in French; its A side,
Mack the Knife, was German.
I don't know anymore
where anything begins or ends.

*

People had assembled for a party.
We had heard there'd be a band.
The band was late, the night adrift.
Thinking of nothing,
I picked up a dead electric guitar, and
face to the wall, fingered a blues in E.
When someone turned on the amp I jumped,
then turned to see the room erupt in dancing.
I held the rhythm as long as I could,
which was not long, then, terrified, fled.
I regret the times I've been unable
to rise to the occasion.

After Simon and Garfunkel split up,
Paul Simon changed the keys to all his tunes.
I'm tired of writing songs, he said,
for Art Garfunkel to sing.
But when they played together
in Central Park years later,
the songs were back in Art's key,
and Paul Simon never looked nor sounded
so radiant.

*

Bob Dylan wanted to be the next Elvis.
Like so many of my generation,
I once wanted to be the next Bob Dylan.
He came closer to his mark, of course,
but when I hear those lovesick songs he's made lately,
some days I'm not so sure.

In the Lake Superior Winter

an ice road is formed
to drive from island to mainland.

Six inches of ice can hold a car over water two hundred feet deep.

I slowly move across.
The tires over stiff snow creak:
shipwreck shipwreck shipwreck

The boys build an oval race track

and in their junk cars   circle and play

performing dazzling spins and turns

they collide   slide   into nothing

Some years a crack opens
swallowing the occasional truck or Cadillac.

A couple from the city tried to move a house across
attached to the back of a semi.

Fish now swim in its kitchen.

Au Musée du Quai Branly

". . . they were never wrong, the Old Masters."
W H. Auden

The finger that points
at the moon
is not the moon.

The West,
standing before the objects
its hand has grasped
from the moon,
contemplates its finger.

It invites
the descendants
of the inhabitants
of the moon
to join it in the exercise.

"Why am I here?"
asks the novelist from Martinique.
"Why was I invited?"
says the philosopher from Ghana.

The moon, from here,
appears
very distant.

Even its inhabitants
perceive its features
with difficulty,
as if
through glass.

Le Cri du Monde

à petits pas de cicatrice mal fermée/
with small steps like a scar poorly closed.

Aimé Césaire

Singer to public sang
fa
fa
mi
fa
fa

Dancer to singer turned
and told
of a thousand laments in the bend of a back, of unfathomed force
in the feel of a foot on the earth, this soil, this toil, history's roil
in the writhe of a wrist, a phantom hymn in the lift of a limb,
pulsed in a pose, secreted in a syllable

Fa
Fa
Fa
Mi
Fa

          Farther
than your voice can carry   I carry
this scarred body my heavy country bends bound bounded
wounded winds here winds up here cannot sing cannot take wing
cannot win here how here? spine spins splits splayed open here
orphan pain pining here breathes fear bends back bent back bent

FA
FA
FA

MI
FA
      Farther
than your vision can reach   I seek
a soul's leap in the arc of an arm, a landscape limned
in the nape of a neck a people's past rythming a spin
a future forms in the weave of a space in the turn
of a race in the dare of a dream breaking out breaking bounds
bursting birthing open here landscape and limb memory
and dream unfolding claiming proclaiming here

FA!
FA!
FA!

      a surging force sweeping forward   F—
      leaves faceless silence behind

      a furious voice foiled here

        space
        contained

        fades

          farther

            fades

dancer to silence turned
and turned
mourned

mourned

fade

(fa

French Lesson #8: La Phonétique

Papa   *part*   *pour*   *Paris*

Papa is leaving for Paris

Papa   departs

softly   a whisper

see

how the flame

barely flickers

Papa   *part*   *pour*   *paradis*

softly   departing

leave

a candle burning

Thank You for Crawling

Your fall is unimportant to us. Due to the unusually heavy volume
of newly transferred wealth, we are experiencing significant delight.
Stay in line, and one of our agents will deal with you curtly.
Your good fortune will be manhandled
in the disorder we've unleashed.

To help us better unnerve you in the future,
this collapse may be monitored for taming purposes.
To expedite your falter, you may choose from the following rejections.
Please pay attention, as obligations have changed.

Para espagnol, leave this country. Go home.
To review your account decimation, enter 401k.
To report a lost or stolen future, hang up and try again later.
If you would like to make a payment, press zero,
our fast operators are standing by to assail you.
Please have your carte blanche ready.
To speak with a representative,
a large campaign donation is required.
Press Fortune 500.

To return to the pain menu, stay online.
Get hung up.
Roll for seven, and
wish upon a star.

The Washing-Machine Stream

The stream that winter
looked like a front-loading washer—
water and foam under a sheer layer of ice
surging
while our faces at the window,
despite the cold,
stared hypnotized.

How can I look at that stream now? Fred said.
You've desecrated the landscape.
As if I had dumped a hulking Maytag
onto the rocks of Gooseberry Falls.

We watched the washing-machine stream
run down to Lake Superior,
carrying away our impurities,
depositing them there.

All these years later
in some overlit laundromat
I think of that window, that surging.
Of all the rivers we walked that winter,
this is the one I remember.

Last Poem

For Laura P.

I wish I knew why you left early,
just as the gathering was swelling to fullness.
When the host announced you had gone,
we were stunned into pained and awkward silence.
Since you were the reason
I was there at all, I considered leaving, too.
But ever the dutiful daughter, as you'd say,
out of impotence, or politeness, I stayed.

Slowly the wine and time did the trick.
A quick joke here, an anecdote there,
and soon the evening was flowing again.
Will you forgive me? I even danced,
and laughed as we licked the last juices
from the bursting red berry dessert.

Outside the night waited,
then grew tired of waiting,
and went about its business in the dark.

I finally left alone.
With my brain on fire and my chest burning
from a last dose of *eau de vie*,
I unsteadily made my way home.
The wet grass, the cool night air, the sound of wind like a river
awakened me.

I wonder now what will transpire,
the complicated reckoning that awaits us.

Copy Book

Because the day's grayness as yet has no shape,
because wresting form from this morning
will require much heavy lifting, more
than I have the heart or the muscle for;
because I see in these lines something sinuous
and hard, a rigor I have come to admire,
even in my ignorance of its workings;
because I have, like dried bean or lentils,
little flavor of my own but benefit
from strong company (*have you been
spending time with Kathy Regan again*
my mother would say, noting her distinctive rhythms
marking my monkey ear speech); and finally,
perhaps, because I love their somber sadness in my mouth,
with a pen and notebook I start to record, whole,
moving solemnly down my page,
the poems of Jack Gilbert's *Refusing Heaven.*
A certain way of paying attention. A caress
that lingers with the slowness love requires.

The Need for Building

Finally
>October arrives
>relieving us of the need for building

Too late
>says the sting of frost on your fingers
>gloveless in the glittering sun

Fine
>you reply thinking this will free you
>of dreams you only half-wanted anyway

It's about time
>says your lover who has waited all summer
>for nothing but you to return

Indeed it is
>you say kissing your lover
>taking your time

With you
>when you leave

Vilnius Courtyard Parade

Savage parade of courtyards   scar that made this green space.
Pile of bricks behind it the silenced family bickering—
Dirty bourgeois bedbugs! Salt . . . pepper up your nose!
Better not to speak of it. Owls amid the ruins,
today's a violent paradise in the wake of master jugglers
transforming the place and the people.
An old woman on a bench droning like a radio.
A young mother paces, baby on hip phone at her ear.
Men mumbling around a bin. These scenes do not intersect.
Terrors last . . . could go on for months.
Tomorrow, who knows, to the dogs.
Yesterday the silence of a majestic cat.

French Lesson #3: Le Temps du verbe

1. *Le présent*
The present is tense.

2. *Le passé composé*
The past compounds our problems. Completed actions require an auxiliary. We all need help when putting together the past.

To be—without object. In transit between birth and death. To rise. To fall. To stay or leave.

Or, to have—direction, an objective. Having, always taking.

Choose one of these to assist you.

3. *L'imparfait*
Memory is imperfect, as we've been over. Whether the day was yellow or red, however vivid the cinders—imperfect. Streets of your childhood, the air in that house, diffuse, like fog.

The list of imperfections is long:
    emotional states—I was afraid
    static conditions—we didn't know   we weren't able
    repeated behaviors—every year we used to . . .
                again and again he would . . .

actions interrupted, secondary players hovering in the
background, all imperfect:

what were you doing when
—name your cohort's catastrophe here—
                    Kennedy was shot the Challenger blew

were you dancing were you sleeping when
        the towers fell
        the waters rose
        the bombs began landing in Baghdad
we were sleeping we were dreaming we were
just so tired from working
when the music halted   the curtain ripped

4. *Le plus-que-parfait*
But to have had—more than perfect.
Before the past that was.

5. *Le futur proche*
The future is near. It is approaching.
I am going
to go.

Here, After

You didn't expect to live even this long.
Not that you have to wake
thanking someone for your days.
They are simply days—cold in the house
in winter, summer rain on the roof.
But this passion, so naked, unexpected,
wasn't this worth staying for?

I am inhabited by your future absence.
I wonder if that's what love means.
Were I younger, it would mean:
I'll be leaving soon. But now
when you love me all night,
there is no need to play at darkness.
We are bearing down on heaven
with green days growing thin. I don't flinch.

Notes

Household: Object Lesson: The diary entry by Virginia Woolf was written three weeks before her death.

Au Musée du Quai Branly: "The finger that points . . ." Buddhist saying displayed on the museum entrance ramp, part of the installation "L'autre marche" (The Other Walk), by Trinh T Minh Ha and Jean-Paul Bordier, June 2006-June 2009.

Le Cri du monde: After the performance by the Québecois dance troupe, Compagnie Marie Chouinard, Pittsburgh, February 2004.

For all the recent springs in the world, and for those pushed back.

French Lesson #8: "Papa . . ." An old trick to teach the pronunciation of the soft French [p] was to hold a lit match in front of one's mouth while pronouncing this phrase. This poem is in memory of my father.

Vilnius Courtyard Parade: This poem includes lines from *Promise at Dawn* by Romain Gary and "Parade" by Arthur Rimbaud.

Deep gratitude goes to all the poets and teachers who have generously labored to make this work better: Michael Wurster, Jan Beatty, Stacey Waite and Joy Katz, for their inspiration, guidance and encouragement; Joan Bauer, Jill Khoury, Daniela Bucilli and Michelle Maher for their attentive reading and good company; Rick St. John for the care he takes with everything. I am grateful, too, to the vibrant poetry communities of Pittsburgh: Joan and Jimmy for keeping language alive at Hemingway's; Romella Kitchens for her equanimity; the Madwomen for their boldness and energy; the Pittsburgh Poetry Exchange for being open to all. Special thanks to Tom Underiner for his knowledge of visual language. Finally, boundless thanks to Ruth Hendricks, photographer extraordinaire and even better friend, midwife to this book.

Roberta Hatcher's poetry has appeared in *St. Petersburg Review, Main Street Rag, Comstock Review* and *The Pittsburgh Post-Gazette*, among others. She was a finalist for the Patricia Dobler Poetry Award and the Arkadii Dragomoshchenko Prize for innovative use of language in poetry. Her poem "French Lesson #3" was nominated for Best New Poets 2014. She holds a Ph.D. in French from the University of Wisconsin-Madison and has taught French language and francophone postcolonial studies at several universities. She has also worked variously as a bartender, waitress, forestry camp worker, cook, au pair, student tour operator and ESL tutor. She currently makes her home in Pittsburgh, PA.

CPSIA information can be obtained at www.ICGtesting.com
Printed in the USA
BVOW06s1144300816

460567BV00003B/9/P